People Who Help Us

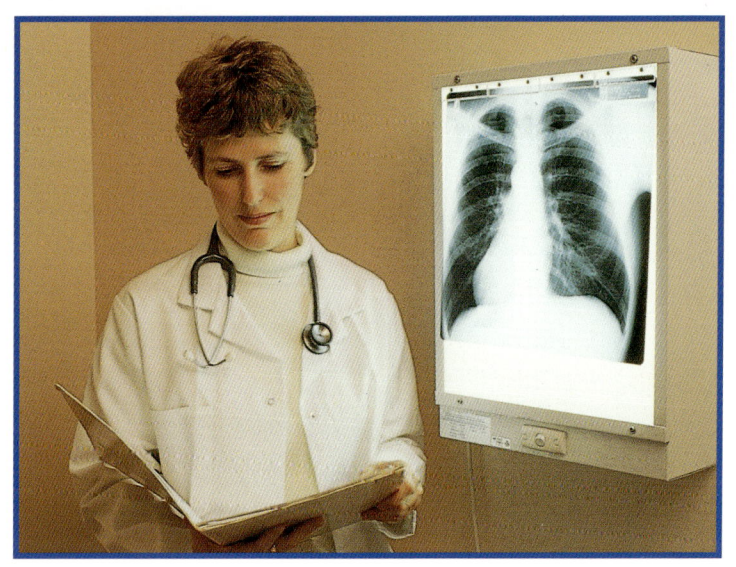

Written by Paul Reeder

Photographed by Damon McPhail

I can see a firefighter at the fire station.

2

I can see a teacher at the school.

3

I can see a mechanic
at the garage.

I can see a police officer at the police station.

5

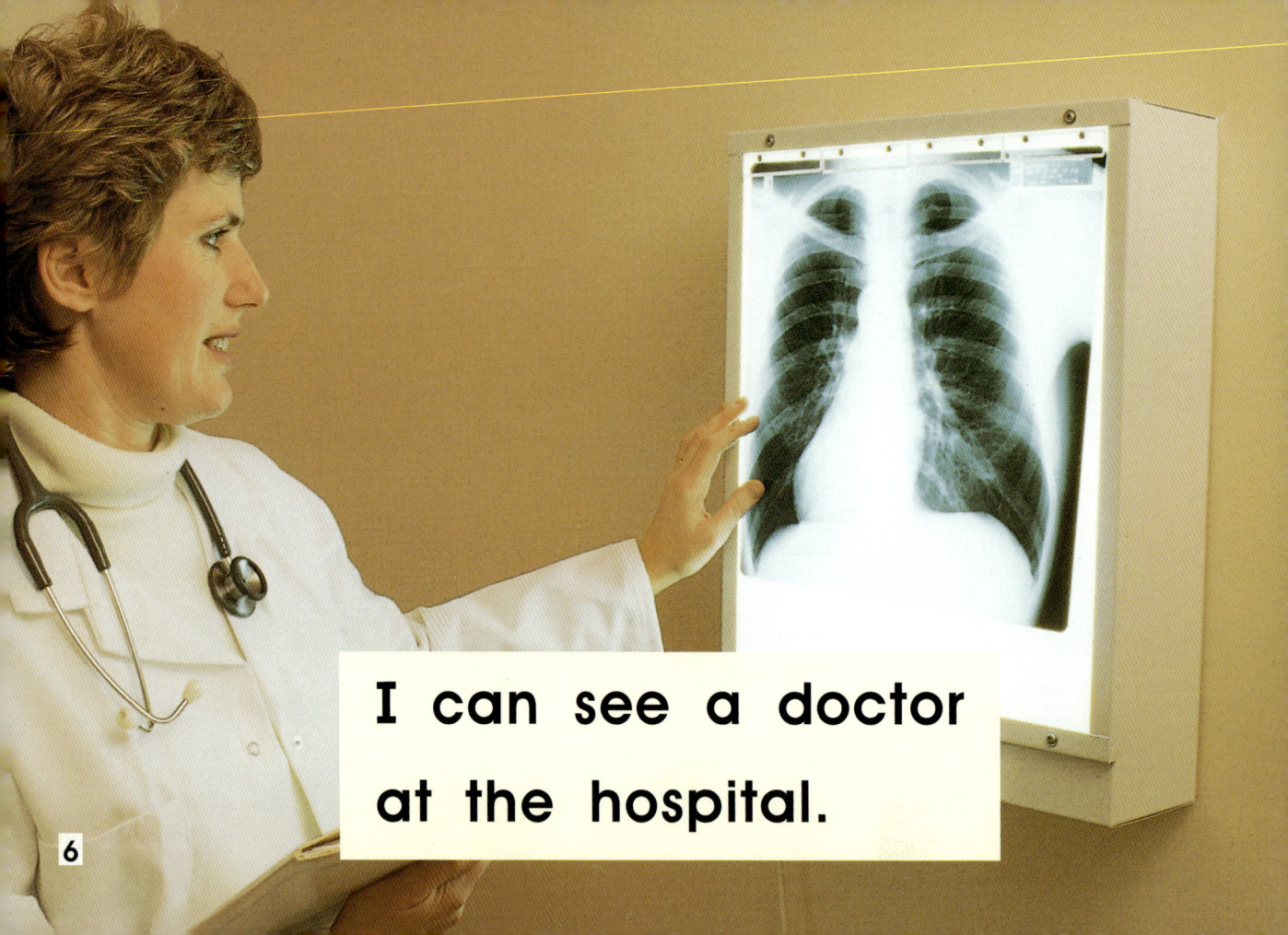

I can see a doctor
at the hospital.

6

I can see a checkout clerk at the store.

7

I can see a bus driver at the bus stop.